WHOEVER WINS...
WE LOSE.

ALIEN VS. PREDATOR™

CIVILIZED BEASTS

STORY

MIKE KENNEDY

PENCILS

ROGER ROBINSON

COLORS

CHARLIE KIRCHOFF

LETTERING

MICHAEL D. THOMAS

COVER ART

ROGER ROBINSON

DARK HORSE BOOKS®

PUBLISHER
Mike Richardson

EDITOR

Chris Warner

PUBLICATION DESIGN
Stephen Reichert

SPECIAL THANKS TO
Debbie Olshan
AT TWENTIETH CENTURY FOX LICENSING

PUBLISHED BY

Dark Horse Books
A division of Dark Horse Comics, Inc.
10956 SE Main Street
Milwaukie, OR 97222

www.darkhorse.com

First edition: March 2008

ISBN 978-1-59307-342-8

1 3 5 7 9 10 8 6 4 2

Printed in China

THERE ARE TWO SCHOOLS ON THE TOPIC OF CIVILIZATION--
ONE PROFESSES THAT IT IS ACHIEVED THROUGH EVOLUTION...
...THE ACCIDENTAL BYPRODUCT OF CONTINUED SURVIVAL.

SHOULD ANY SPECIES EVOLVE TO THE POINT OF ORGANIZED SENTIENCE, EITHER THROUGH COMMUNAL BEHAVIOR OR DOMINANCE, IT CAN BE CONSIDERED "CIVILIZED".
THE OTHER SCHOOL, HOWEVER, DEFINES CIVILIZATION AS A PLANNED, INTENTIONAL STRUCTURE.
A BODY OF LAWS CREATED TO INSURE SURVIVAL.

WHILE THESE SCHOOLS MAY DISAGREE ON THE MERIT OF THE CONCEPT...
WHETHER IT BE ACCIDENTAL OR INTENTIONAL...
...THEY DO AGREE ON ONE ASPECT--
THE PIVOTAL SIGNIFICANCE OF *DOMINION*.

IT IS THE UNIVERSAL FULCRUM ON WHICH ALL LIFE BALANCES--
SHANK
--SOVEREIGNTY VS. SURVIVAL--
--INTELLECT VS. INSTINCT--
--DOMINION VS. DEATH...
BLAM!

...FOR IN THE END, EVERYTHING FALLS INTO ONE CATEGORY OR THE OTHER.
VICTOR OR VICTIM.
NNN... NGH...
SSSSSSSSSS
ARE YOU OKAY?!?

GET IT OFF, GET IT OFF--
DID HE GET YOU?!?
...LITTLE BIT...
HOLD STILL, DON'T TOUCH IT --
...NICE SHOOTIN'... YOU BEEN PRACTIC-ING...?
NOT ENOUGH AMMO LEFT TO WASTE ON PRACTICE. JUST TRYING TO MAKE EACH SHOT COUNT...
...GOOD JOB...

HSSSSSSSSSSS
LOOK OUT--!

...CRAP.

JUST RELAX... IT'S GOOD HERE... WE DON'T WANT ANY TROUBLE...
...DROP THE SPEAR...
IF HE SWINGS, I SWING.
IF HE SWINGS, IT WON'T MATTER. PUT IT DOWN...

AHHDAMMIT--!
HEY! HEYHEYHEY HEY--!!!
...HEYYYY, THAT'S NIIIIIIICE...
THANKS FOR THE HELP, SMILEY.
YOUR MOTHER IS A WHORE...
YOUR MOTHER IS A WHORE...
HOW DOES HE KNOW?
WATCH IT. SHE'S YOUR MOTHER, TOO...

WELL THAT WAS PRETTY LUCKY, EH? SMILEY SHOWING UP LIKE THAT...
I WOULDN'T CALL IT LUCK...
WELL, WHATEVER YOU WANNA CALL IT, I'M GRATEFUL FOR IT.
WE SHOULD FOLLOW HIM SOME-TIME, MAYBE BRING HIM A PIE OR SOMETHING...
I DOUBT HE'D LET US ANYWHERE NEAR HIS CAMP.
WE'LL NEVER KNOW UNTIL WE TRY...
I TRIED. END OF STORY.
YOU DID? WHEN?
HEY! YOU'RE BACK!

OH, NO-- WHAT HAPPENED? ARE YOU OKAY?!
I'M FIIIIIINE, REALLY... SMILEY'S GOT THE BEST DRUGS...
WELCOME BACK. HOW'D IT GO?
IT'S DEAD. WE GOT IT.
WELL, SMILEY GOT IT, BUT WE HURT IT PRETTY GOOD FIRST.
INTERESTING. WHAT'S THAT, THE THIRD HUNT HE'S SHOWN UP...?
BUT THE FIRST TIME HE EVER HELPED.
FIRST TIME WE NEEDED HELP...

WELL, MAYBE HE COULD HELP WITH THE TILLING, SEEING AS HOW THE REST OF YOU'D RATHER STAND AROUND FLAPPING YOUR MOUTHS.
I'D LIKE TO FINISH BEFORE DARK...
RELAX, GLENDA, YOU'RE GONNA GIVE YOUSELF AN ANEURISM.
RELAX?!? WE'VE BEEN STRANDED ON THIS ROCK FOR EIGHT MONTHS! OUR SUPPLIES RAN OUT WEEKS AGO, THE WOODS ARE FULL OF MONSTERS, AND YOU TELL ME TO RELAX?!?
GETTING UPTIGHT ISN'T GONNA MAKE THINGS ANY BETTER--
WELL THEY CAN'T GET MUCH WORSE.
IF I HAD KNOWN YOU WERE GONNA RUIN OUR LIVES LIKE THIS, I'D HAVE PACKED MORE HAPPY PILLS.

...SO IT'S CLEARLY NOT TIED TO A LUNAR CYCLE...
PIG--!
YOU KNOW, IT'S NOT JUST GLENDA WHO FEELS THAT WAY...
A LOT OF THEM ARE GETTING MORE AND MORE STRESSED OUT OVER THIS MESS.
MOST OF THE CAMP BELIEVES WE'RE JUST WAITING OUT A *DEATH SENTENCE*.
OH, HEY... SORRY, MAN. THEY DON'T *ALL* BLAME YOU.
WELL, THAT'S NICE TO HEAR.

AW, C'MON... IT'S ONLY BEEN *EIGHT MONTHS.*
RESCUE'S GOTTA BE ON ITS WAY. ANY DAY NOW, JUST WATCH...
WAKE UP, SHANE. IT SHOULD ONLY TAKE *SIX* MONTHS TO GET HERE.
...SIX MONTHS AND *SIXTY BILLION DOLLARS*...

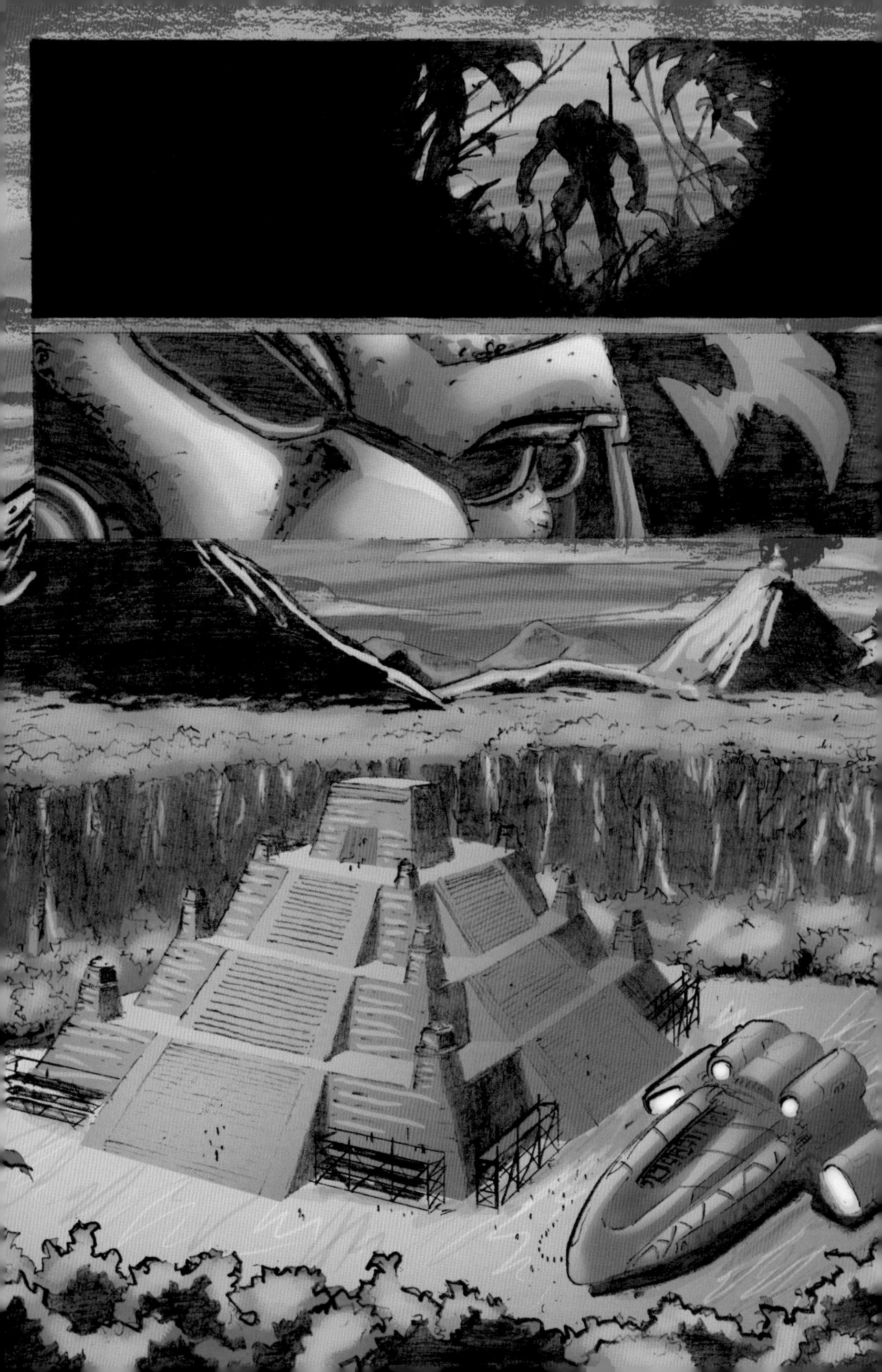

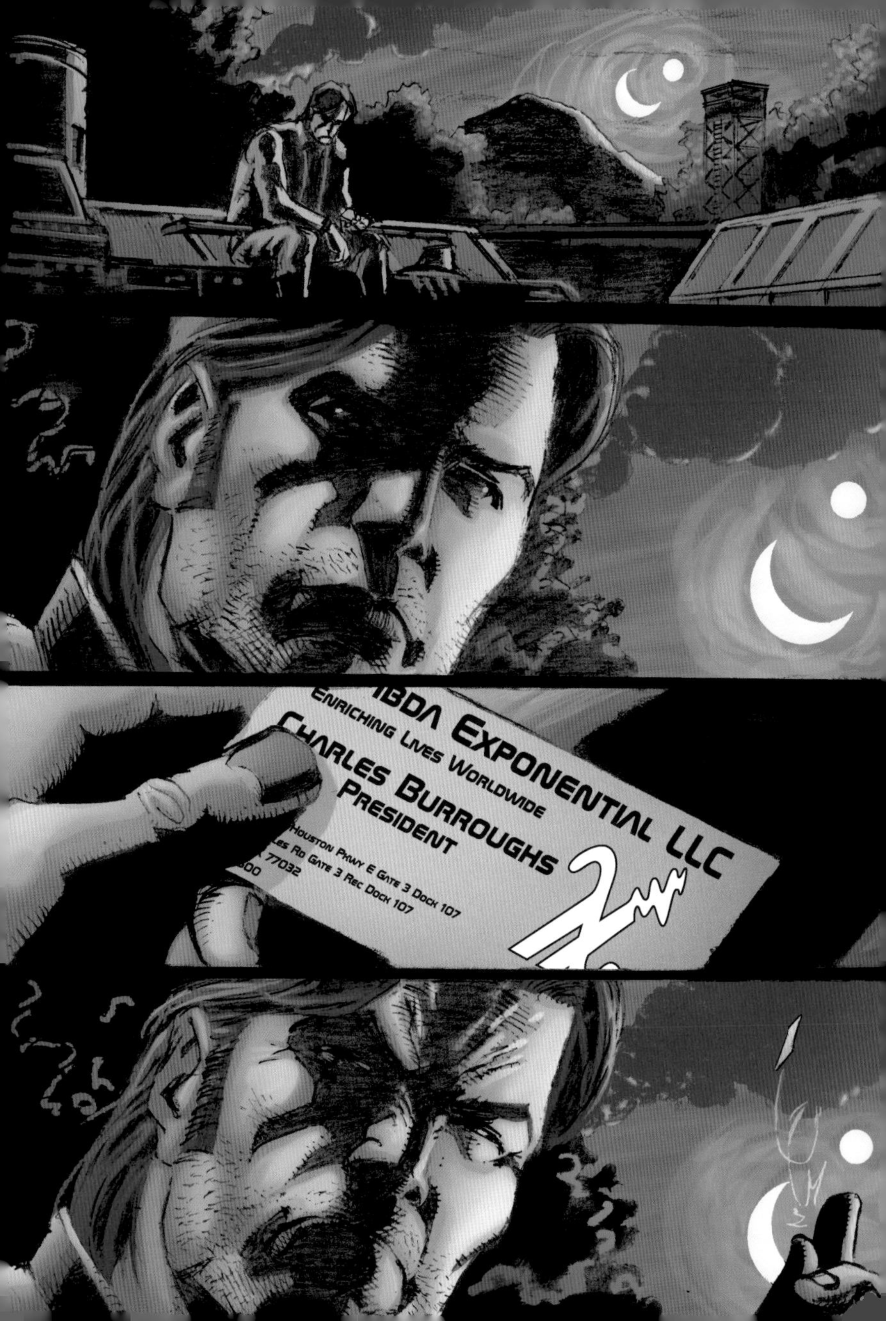
EXPONENTIAL LLC
ENRICHING LIVES WORLDWIDE
CHARLES BURROUGHS
PRESIDENT
HOUSTON PKWY E GATE 3 DOCK 107
RD GATE 3 REC DOCK 107
77032

HOT *DAMN*...
WHAT TOOK YOU GUYS SO LONG??
SORRY FOR THE DELAY. UNUSUAL CIRCUM-STANCES.

CHUCK, THIS IS A BUSINESS PARTNER OF MINE, *TYLER TEMPLETON.* WE GO WAY BACK, ME AND HIM...
MR. BURROUGHS, IT'S AN HONOR...
...YEAH, SAME... *ER*...
...MAC, IS THAT *YOUR* LOGO ON THE HULL? SINCE WHEN DOES *STEED CORONA* HAVE INTERPLANETARY CAPABILITY?
SINCE YOU INVITED ME ON THIS WEEKEND TOUR. I FIGURED WE MIGHT END UP PARTNERS IN THIS DEAL, SO I COVERED MY BETS.
WHY DIDN'T YOU SAY ANYTHING??
LIKE WHAT? ALL I DID WAS PUT A FEW PURCHASE ORDERS IN THE PIPE BEFORE I LEFT. I HAD NO IDEA THEY'D GO THROUGH SO QUICK. I'M JUST AS GLAD TO SEE THEM AS YOU ARE...
THEY COULD BE LITTLE GREEN MEN FOR ALL I CARE. JUST TAKE US BACK HOME!
WE HAVE TO HURRY. GRAB ONLY WHAT'S ESSENTIAL. WE NEED TO DUST OFF BEFORE THE WARSHIP RETURNS FROM ORBIT.

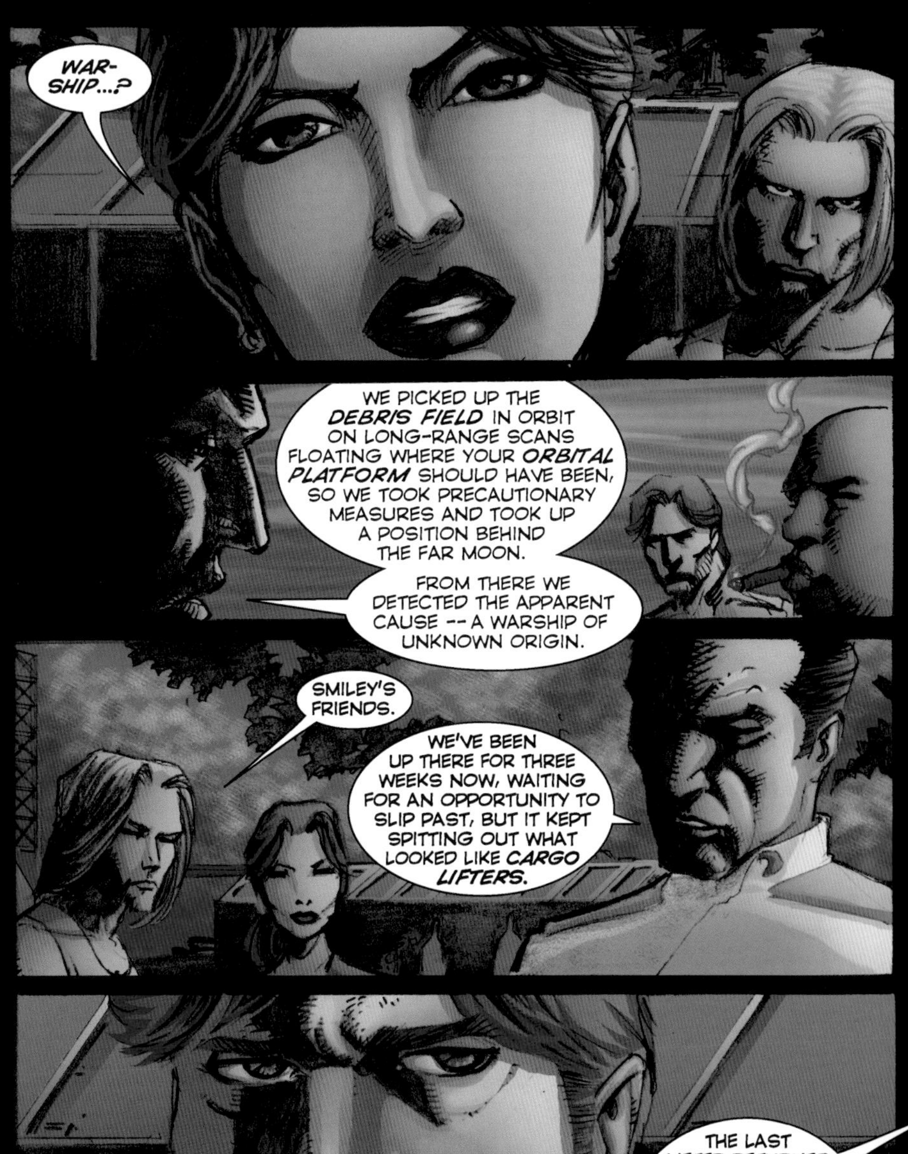
WAR-SHIP...?
WE PICKED UP THE DEBRIS FIELD IN ORBIT ON LONG-RANGE SCANS FLOATING WHERE YOUR ORBITAL PLATFORM SHOULD HAVE BEEN, SO WE TOOK PRECAUTIONARY MEASURES AND TOOK UP A POSITION BEHIND THE FAR MOON.
FROM THERE WE DETECTED THE APPARENT CAUSE -- A WARSHIP OF UNKNOWN ORIGIN.
SMILEY'S FRIENDS.
WE'VE BEEN UP THERE FOR THREE WEEKS NOW, WAITING FOR AN OPPORTUNITY TO SLIP PAST, BUT IT KEPT SPITTING OUT WHAT LOOKED LIKE CARGO LIFTERS.

THE LAST LIFTER RETURNED YESTERDAY, AND THE WARSHIP TOOK OFF ON A GENERAL ORBIT PATTERN. WHATEVER THEY WERE DOING DOWN HERE, THEY SEEM TO BE DONE.

ASSUMING IT CONTINUES AT ITS CURRENT SPEED, WE'VE GOT ABOUT *THREE HOURS* TO DUST OFF.
THEN LET'S GET CRACKING. SHANE, HOW MUCH DATA CAN YOU BUNDLE UP IN A HURRY?
I'LL START BURNING BACKUPS. GIMME AN HOUR.
THIRTY MINUTES.
I'LL HELP.
GLENDA SAYS WE'RE GOING HOME... IS THAT TRUE??
LOOKS THAT WAY.
PACK UP EVERYTHING ESSENTIAL AND SENSITIVE...
...VACATION'S OVER.

SKREEEEEEEEEEEEEEE

SSSSSSSSSSSSSSSSSSSSSS

SKREEEEEEEEEEEEEEEEEEE!

SKREEEEEEEEEEEEEEEEEE!!

TEMPLETON, HOW ARE WE DOING ON TIME?
WE'LL BE FINE AS LONG AS WE KEEP MOVING.
WE'RE ALMOST SET. SAY... LET ME ASK YOU SOME-THING--
HOW DID YOU KNOW WHERE TO FIND US? OR THAT WE EVEN *NEEDED* A RESCUE?
MR. MACARTHUR SHARED WHAT LITTLE INFORMATION YOU PROVIDED SO WE COULD DESIGN OUR TRANSPORTATION ACCORDINGLY.
WE REALLY ARE LOOKING FORWARD TO *PARTNERING* WITH YOU HERE.
I GET THAT, BUT MAC NEVER MENTIONED HE HAD A RESCUE CONTINGENCY...
WELL, HE DIDN'T REALLY.
NOT THAT HE COULD COUNT ON, AT LEAST.
AFTER ELEVEN WEEKS OF SILENCE, WE CON-TACTED YOUR PEOPLE AT LAMBDA EXPONENTIAL.
YOUR PR SPECIALISTS ARE QUITE... *OBSTINATE,* IF I MAY BE FRANK.
AT A LOSS FOR CON-CLUSIVE INFORMATION, WE DECIDED TO COME AND SEE WHAT WAS HAPPENING FOR OURSELVES.
GOOD THING, TOO...

UNIT GROUP, CODE NINE --
WAIT!!

...WHAT...?

NO! STOP!! WHAT'S HAPPENING?!
HELP! SOME-BODY!!
CHARLES, DO SOME-THING!
PLEASE, FOR GOD'S SAKE--
--ANYBODY!!!

BACK OFF, SMILEY!
SHE'S WITH ME!
SHANE, DON'T--!
WE'RE NOT CAUSING TROUBLE--!
SHANE, SIT DOWN...
SCREW THAT...
SHANE--
>GK< --

TRY THAT CRAP WITH ME...
WAIT. LET'S NOT ESCALATE MATTERS...
WHAT THE HELL ARE YOU DOING?

WELL, THIS IS JUST SPIFFY...
I THINK I JUST LOST MY BUZZ...

WHERE DO YOU THINK THEY'RE HEADED?
I DOUBT IT'S *DINNER* AND *A MOVIE*...
UNLESS *THEY'RE* THE DINNER...
IF WE CAN GET OUTSIDE THE CAMP, WE CAN TRACK TEMPLETON WITHIN A SQUARE YARD.
IS HE WEARING A LOCATOR?
SOME-THING LIKE THAT...

INTER-
ESTING...
SOMETHING ON YOUR MIND, TEMPLETON?
ELEMENTS IN THE ARCHITECTURE ARE FAMILIAR, BUT THE GLYPHS ARE INCON-SISTENT... PARTS OF IT ARE VERY TERRESTRIAL, BUT... OTHER PARTS AREN'T...
I READ DATAFILES ABOUT SOMETHING LIKE THIS BEFORE THE *BIG DELETION*...
BEFORE...? THAT WAS A *HUNDRED YEARS AGO*...
YOU KNOW WHAT I MEAN. I'VE BEEN OFFWORLD A LONG TIME...
I THOUGHT YOU LAUNCHED FROM EARTH.
WE DID.
THEN WHEN WERE YOU OFF-WORLD?
BEFORE THAT.

HOW OLD *ARE* YOU??
OLDER THAN I LOOK.
SO, WHAT... ARE WE ARRESTED OR SOMETHING? WHAT DID WE SUPPOSEDLY DO?
THIS ISN'T A PRISON.
WHAT THEN?
IF I HAD TO GUESS, BASED ON THE SIZE AND HEIGHT OF THE TABLES, I'D SAY AN INFIRMARY. OR A *MORGUE*.
BUT I'D ONLY BE GUESSING.

WHAT ARE WE GOING TO DO?
WE'RE NOT GOING TO PANIC... THEY HAVEN'T HURT US YET. WE MIGHT BE JUMPING TO CON-CLUSIONS...
WHAT'RE YOU GUYS UP TO?
IF YOU'RE GOING TO *MAKE A MOVE,* I WANT IN.
DON'T TAKE THIS WRONG, SHANE, BUT YOU'RE NOT IN THEIR LEAGUE...
WHAT'S *THAT* SUPPOSED TO MEAN?

...WHO IN HELL *ARE* THESE GUYS...?
YOU ALL COMING OR NOT?!?

WE CAN'T JUST LEAVE THEM BACK THERE TO DIE! WHOSE DUMB-ASS IDEA WAS THAT??
THEY KNEW WHAT THEY WERE DOING...
WHAT ARE THEY, MAC? GENE-BUILDS? N-TRANS ADDICTS?
COME ON, MAN--THEY'RE *SYNTHETICS!* FIGURED THAT'D BE OBVIOUS...
BUT THEY *BLEED RED*...
EASY ADJUSTMENT, HELPS THEM BLEND IN BETTER...
HOLD ON... YOU'RE *BUILDING* THEM?! SYNTHS ARE *ILLEGAL!!* HAVE BEEN SINCE *THE DELETION!*

WHY DO YOU THINK WE'RE KEEPING THEM A SECRET?
LOOK... SYNTHETICS WERE NEVER THE PROBLEM. HUMAN PARANOIA WAS THE PROBLEM. WE BUILT THEM TOO SMART, AND THAT SCARED TOO MANY PEOPLE. WE CREATED THE VIRUS THAT CAUSED THE BIG DELETION.
WE BUILT IT TO HUNT THEM DOWN AND KILL THEM WHEREVER THEY HID, AND IT CAME BACK TO BITE US ON THE ASS, WIPE OUT EVERY COM-PUTER SYSTEM WE EVER BUILT.
OUR *FEAR* DID THAT, NOT THEM.
THAT DOESN'T CHANGE THE FACT THAT YOU'RE BREAKING ABOUT A HUNDRED LAWS! IS THAT WHY YOU CAME OUT HERE? TO SET UP AN ILLEGAL SYNTH PLANT??
SURE. WHY NOT?
YOU TELLING ME WE CAN'T LEARN FROM A STUPID *MISTAKE?* LEARN TO LIVE WITH ARTIFICIAL INTELLIGENCE WITHOUT *FEARING FOR OUR LIVES?*
THE LAWS GOTTA EVOLVE, MAN. *WE* GOTTA EVOLVE, USE WHAT WE CAN TO REBUILD AGAIN, NOW MORE THAN EVER.
THESE NEW MODELS ARE SUPERIOR IN EVERY WAY -- MORE REASONABLE, MORE NATURAL, MORE USEFUL, MORE INTELLIGENT... MAN, THEY HAD YOU FOOLED...

IT'S NOT ABOUT WHETHER THEY CAN BLEND IN, IT'S ABOUT WHAT THEY CAN *DO!* IF JUST *ONE* OF THEM PICKS UP THE *DELETION VIRUS,* WE COULD FIND OURSELVES BACK IN THE *STONE AGE* ALL OVER AGAIN BEFORE WE'VE EVEN RECOVERED FROM THE *FIRST* WIPE!
I KNOW. THAT'S WHY WE GOTTA KEEP IT A SECRET UNTIL THEY'RE READY. DON'T WANT THE WORLD TO FREAK OUT LIKE YOU JUST DID.
SORRY... NO OFFENSE.
NONE TAKEN.
SO... IS TEMPLE-TON--?
GIVE IT A REST, WILL YA?

WELL, CHARLES...
DON'T --
...HERE'S ANOTHER FINE MESS YOU'VE GOTTEN US INTO...
WHAT DO YOU WANT ME TO SAY, GLENDA? DO YOU WANT ME TO APOLOGIZE? AGAIN?! DO YOU REALLY THINK I KNEW ANY OF THIS COULD HAPPEN?
I'M SURE YOU DIDN'T, AND THAT'S WHERE YOU FAILED! YOU WERE SUPPOSED TO HAVE ALL THE ANGLES COVERED! WE PUT OUR TRUST IN YOU, THREW OUR LIVES BACK HOME INTO STORAGE TO FOLLOW THE "VISIONARY BUSINESSMAN" WHO WAS GONNA "BRING US THE FUTURE"! HA!
GUESS WE KNOW WHO THE REAL FOOLS ARE NOW...
QUIET...
BUTT OUT, EINSTEIN! I DIDN'T SEE YOU DOING MUCH TO HELP BACK THERE EITHER...
SHHH!

WHAT IS THAT? WHAT ARE *THOSE*??
DON'T MOVE AND DON'T MAKE A SOUND...
SHLLLKKKKKKK
AAAAAH--!!

SSSSSSSSSSSSSSSSSss
OH, MY GOD...
THAT EXPLAINS IT...

AAAAAH--!!
...NO...

...NNN...
CLOSE YOUR EYES...
SSSSSSSSSSSSSSSSSSSSSSSSSSSS

YOU'RE A... A...
YES.
HOW DID YOU... WHERE...?
CAN WE DISCUSS THIS LATER?

ABSO-LUTELY. WHAT NOW?

FOLLOW ME.

HOW MUCH FARTHER?
HIS SIGNAL'S CLOSE...
HOW CLOSE?
REAL CLOSE.
OH, CRAP.
ANOTHER ONE?

THIS MUST BE WHAT THEY WERE SENDING DOWN FROM THEIR WARSHIP. THEY WERE *REBUILDING*.
SHANE... WE CAN'T GO IN THERE. THOSE *THINGS*...
IT'S OKAY. STAY OUT HERE WITH THE OTHERS. WE'LL BE BACK OUT BEFORE YOU KNOW IT.
BUT--
WE'LL BE FINE. WE GOT A COUPLE *SUPER SOLDIERS* LEADING THE WAY...
<<...KKAK... S-SSSUPER... SOLDIERS...>>
...YEAH.
WE'LL BE BACK BEFORE YOU KNOW IT.

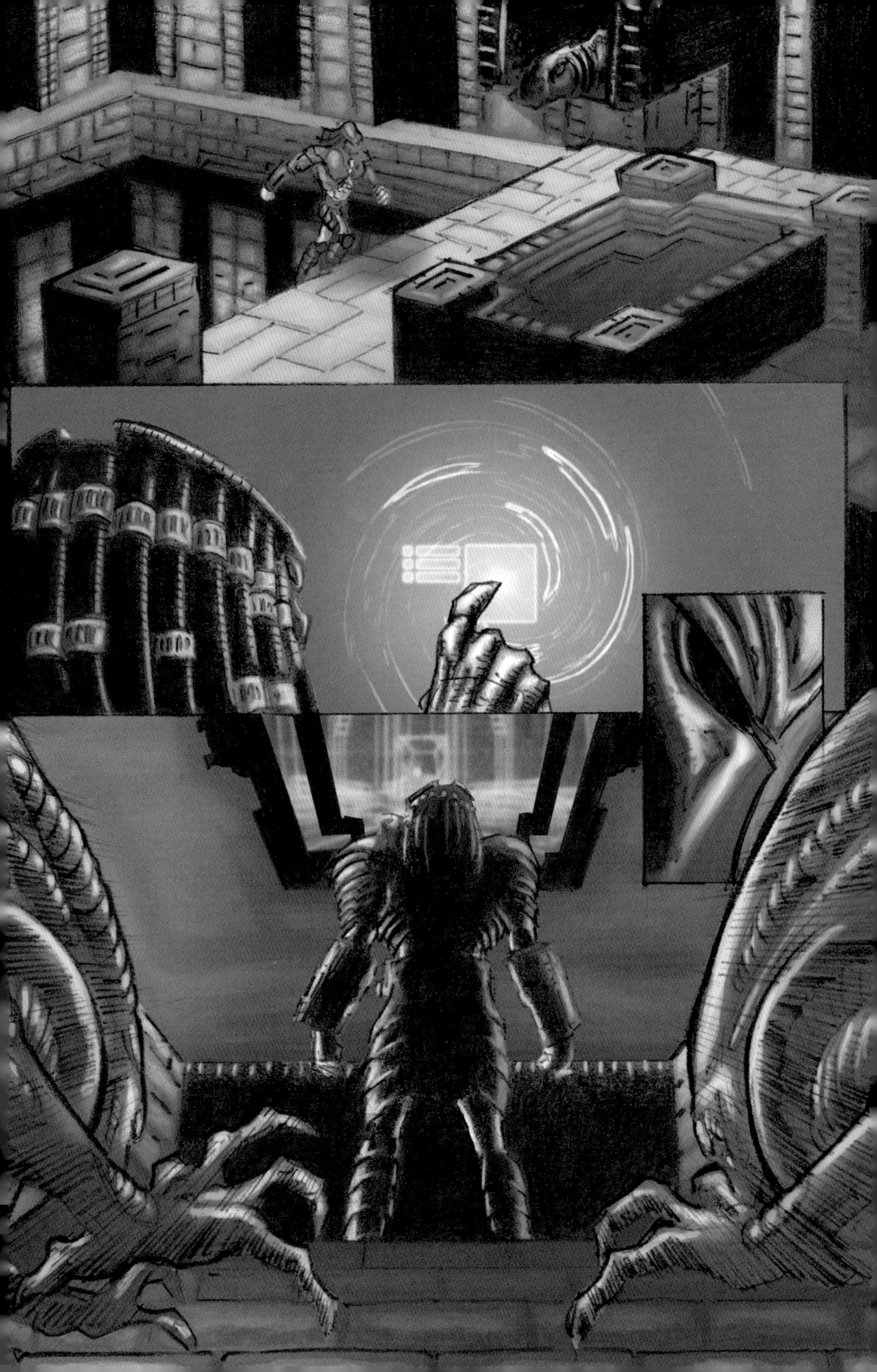

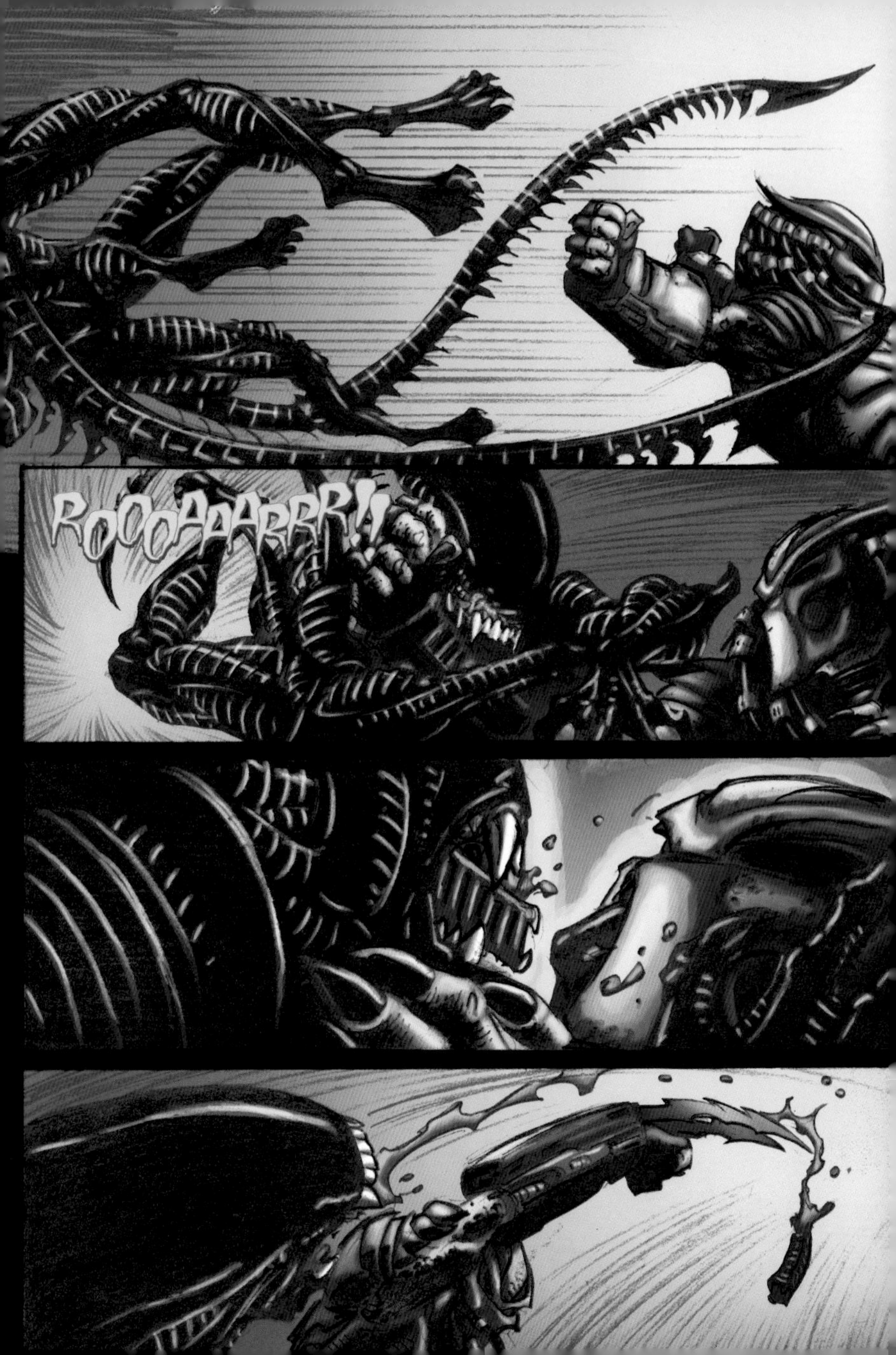
ROOOAAARRRR!!

DO YOU HAVE ANY IDEA WHERE WE'RE HEADED?
MY CREW AND I CAN TRACK EACH OTHER REMOTELY. THEY APPEAR TO BE VERY NEARBY...
GREAT, RESCUED FROM MONSTERS BY KILLER ROBOTS...
YOU'RE MORE THAN WELCOME TO STAY HERE, GLENDA...
WHAT, SO YOU AND YOUR KILLER ROBOT BUDDIES CAN GO OFF AND START *ANOTHER* CIVIL WAR AND MAYBE WIPE OUT WHATEVER COMPUTER SYSTEMS WE MANAGED TO SALVAGE FROM THE *LAST* BIG DELETION...?
WHERE DO YOU GET THESE PARANOID IDEAS OF YOURS?? FOR ONE THING, I HAD *NO IDEA* THEY WERE SYNTHS. AND EVEN IF I DID, RIGHT NOW, *I DON'T CARE!* THEY CAME TO *RESCUE* US! AND YOU'RE GONNA *ARGUE* WITH THAT?!?

RESCUE US, OR TAKE US PRISONER? I DON'T KNOW WHAT VERSION OF HISTORY YOU GOT, BUT LAST I HEARD THOSE BASTARDS TRIED TO KILL US...

IT WAS SELF-DEFENSE.

HMPH. CALL IT WHAT YOU WANT, BUT IT STILL BOILS DOWN TO ONE THING -- A GENOCIDAL BUG IN YOUR SYSTEM.
IF OUR PROGRAMMING WAS FLAWED, WOULDN'T THAT HAVE BEEN YOUR ERROR...?

HOLY...

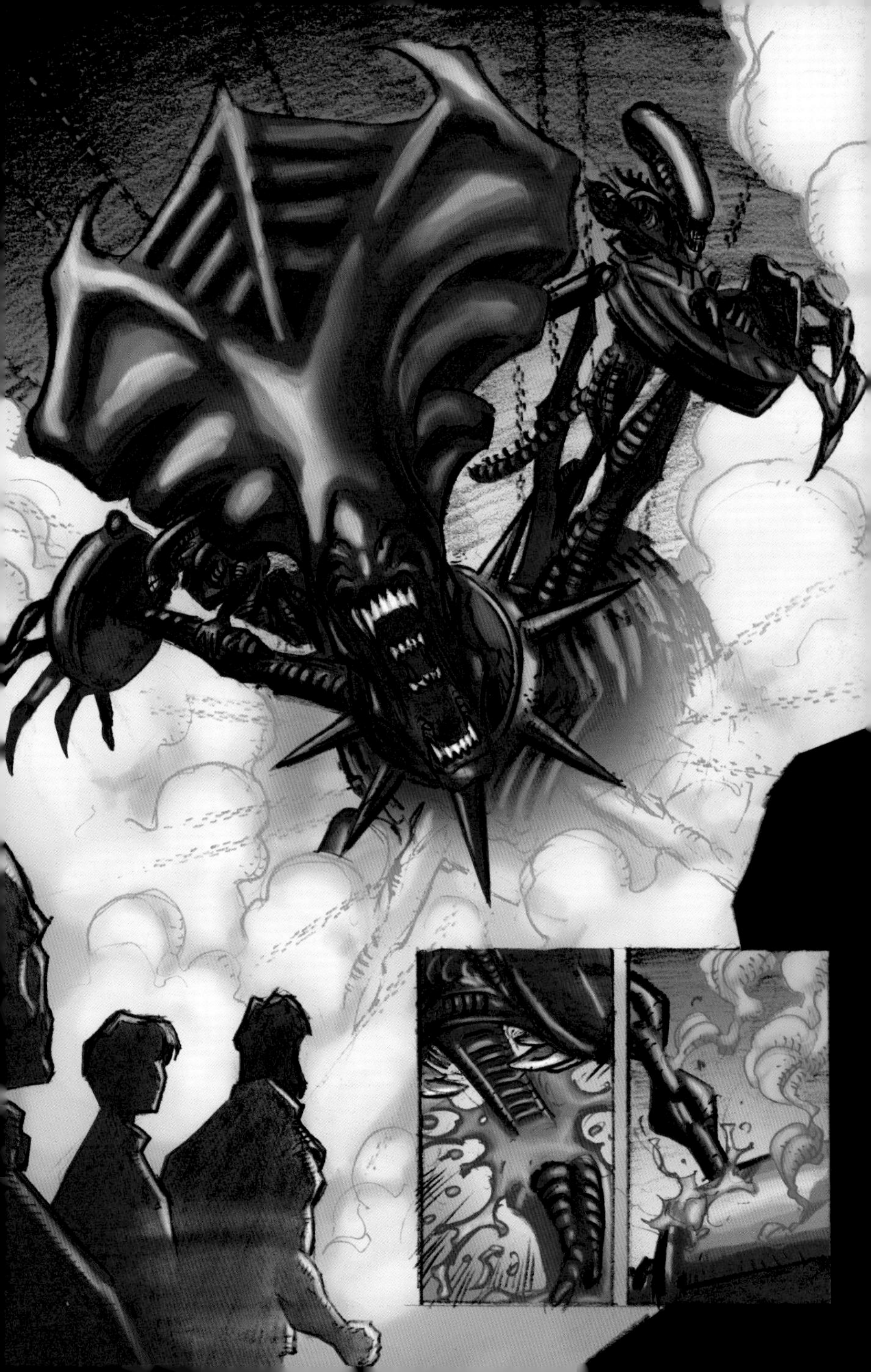

BACK OUT SLOWLY...

GO! GO!

SKREEEEEEEEE--
--EEEERRRR-K-KK-KKK--

HOW DO YOU KNOW THEY'RE NOT GETTING US *LOST?*
'CAUSE I MADE THEM **SMARTER** THAN THAT.
HIS SIGNAL IS VERY CLOSE AND MOVING IN THIS DIRECTION.
SHANE--!
CHARLES...?

HOW'D YOU GET FREE??
WE GOTTA GET THE HELL *OUT OF HERE...*
THE *REDUNDANCY* SHOULD BE ON ITS WAY...
WHAT REDUNDANCY?
AUTOMATED SUPPORT PROTOCOL. IN THE EVENT OF COMMUNICATION FAILURE, ANOTHER DROPSHIP WILL RETURN TO THE LAST KNOWN POSITION.
WE'RE RUNNING SHORT ON TIME. THE WARSHIP WILL BREAK ORBIT IN JUST UNDER AN HOUR.
WE'VE ANOTHER PROBLEM TO CONSIDER AS WELL...

THEY *KNOW.*

YEAH, WE HAD TO REVEAL THE CREW, TOO. ONLY WAY TO GET OUT OF THE CAMP.
WE LOST THREE UNITS.
HOW SHOULD WE PROCEED? IF OUR ENTERPRISE IS EXPOSED BACK ON EARTH, YOU'LL FACE CAPITAL CHARGES, AND THE REST OF US COULD FIND OURSELVES HUNTED AGAIN. IT COULD PLANT THE SEEDS OF ANOTHER WAR.
I HAVE DOUBTS WHETHER WE CAN TRUST OUR SECRET TO REMAIN SO...
WHAT THE HELL ARE YOU GUYS GOING ON ABOUT? WE NEED TO LEAVE...

GET EVERYONE BACK TO THE CAMP! WE'LL COVER YOUR EXIT!
YOU CAN'T TAKE HIM!
YOU DON'T HAVE MUCH TIME. THE RESPONSE TEAM SHOULD BE LANDING SHORTLY, IF THEY AREN'T ALREADY THERE...

ssssSSSSSSSSSSSS

SO HOW LONG WERE YOU GONNA KEEP YOUR SYNTHETIC ENTERPRISE A SECRET, MAC?
I WAS HOPING INDEFINITELY. AT LEAST TILL THEY WERE READY TO SHOW...
DO YOU HAVE ANY IDEA HOW MUCH HOT WATER YOU'LL BE IN -- WE'LL BE IN -- WHEN WE GET BACK TO EARTH?
FED INQUIRY WILL PICK OUR STORY APART, AND THEY WON'T LIKELY BE TOO THRILLED TO HEAR ABOUT ILLEGAL SYNTH ACTIVITY...
WHO SAYS THEY GOTTA KNOW ABOUT THAT PART?
COME ON, MAN... YOU THINK YOU CAN GET EVERYONE HERE TO LIE UNDER OATH FOR YOU?
SERIOUSLY, DO YOU THINK YOU CAN GET GLENDA TO PASS A VK TEST, ASSUMING SHE EVEN AGREES TO TRY...?
HONESTLY...?

...NO, I DON'T THINK SHE COULD.
WHOA, WHAT --??
WHAT THE HELL ARE YOU DOING?!?
WE JUST GOTTA GET EVERYONE INTO ALIGNMENT...
SORRY, CHUCK. I WISH YOU HADN'T FOUND OUT ABOUT THAT STUFF. YOU WERE SUPPOSED TO JUST TAKE THE RIDE HOME NONE THE WISER.

SO WHAT, YOU'RE GONNA *LEAVE* US HERE? TO COVER YOUR OWN ASS?? MIGHT AS WELL JUST *KILL* US THEN...
COME ON, MAN. YOU SAID IT YOURSELF! WHAT CHOICE DO I HAVE? THIS GETS OUT -- AND IT *WILL* -- THESE NEW SYNTHS WON'T HAVE A CHANCE!
IF GLENDA YAPS TO THE MEDIA, THE FEDS, *WHOEVER* -- IT'S *OVER*. NOT JUST FOR *ME*, BUT FOR *THEM*.
I'M LOOKING OUT FOR TWO FUTURES -- *MINE* AND *THEIRS*.

THE WARSHIP WILL BE BREAKING THE HORIZON IN TWENTY MINUTES. IF WE'RE GOING TO LEAVE, WE HAVE TO LEAVE *NOW.*
THEN YOU BETTER GET YOUR PLASTIC ASS ON BOARD.
A third dropship would never make it here without being spotted...
I get that. It's not like I'm enjoying this.

YOU'RE NOT THE MAN I THOUGHT YOU WERE, MAC.
I'M THE MAN *YOU* USED TO BE.

UHNN
SUMMON ANOTHER DROP-SHIP TO THESE COORDINATES, FULL-ENGINE SPEED!
WAIT--!
THE BACKUP WILL BE HERE SHORTLY. BE READY WHEN IT ARRIVES.
WHAT ARE YOU DOING??
RUNNING INTERFERENCE.

IT HAS BEEN SAID THAT HUMANITY'S DOWNFALL BEGAN WITH THE INVEN-TION OF THE WHEEL.
THAT WHEEL WAS OUR ADAM, AND MANKIND'S INSATIABLE CURIOSITY WAS OUR EVE.
FROM THESE MECHANICAL ROOTS, OUR KIND EVOLVED, PERHAPS BEYOND INTENDED LIMITS...
...BUT SUCH IS LIFE.

WHETHER WE GOT HERE BY ACCIDENT OR BY DESIGN, ONE THING IS CERTAIN...
...WE CANNOT GO BACK.
CIVILIZATION IS A GENIE THAT CANNOT BE RE-BOTTLED, NOR CAN IT BE EXTINGUISHED BY ANY MEANS SHORT OF GENOCIDE.
AND SUCH AN EXTREME MEASURE DESTROYS THE VERY FABRIC OF THE CONCEPT.

FOR I BELIEVE THAT CIVILIZATION IS NEITHER AN ACCIDENT NOR A PLAN, BUT RATHER A REWARD BESTOWED ON THOSE WHO LEARN TO WORK WITH THEIR SURROUNDINGS INSTEAD OF AGAINST THEM.
PERHAPS SOMEDAY ALL BEINGS WILL SIT AT THE SAME TABLE WITH EQUAL UNDERSTANDING, BUT UNTIL THEN WE CAN ONLY GUIDE OURSELVES WITH NOBLE INTENTIONS...
...AND HOPE THE REST OF THE UNIVERSE WILL IN TIME LEARN TO DO THE SAME.

®
DARK
HORSE
BOOKS